Team
ReConstruction

Building A
High Performance Work Group
During Change

Price Pritchett

Ron Pound

PRITCHETT

*Productivity is the
true competitive advantage.*

—*Peter Drucker*

Let's not sugarcoat it—you're looking at a tough job.

Restoring productivity and profitability in a work group hit by change doesn't come easy. Employees are distracted, confused, stressed out. Some get angry, some jockey for position. Some simply give up. They're all looking at *you* to "fix things." And even the people who are pumped up and willing to help can't agree on *how* things should be fixed.

Change damages the trust level . . . drives morale south . . . gives organizational loyalty a beating. How can you protect productivity, quality, and profitability under these conditions?

Higher management, meanwhile, is telling you to do more. Do it with less. Do it better. That's the only way the organization can survive in today's competitive environment.

The hard truth? Nobody can say how much time you've got to mobilize this group before you get hit with still *more* changes.

You can't afford to just sit back, let nature take its course, and assume your group will eventually gel into an effective unit. Conventional team-building techniques aren't enough either. They work too slowly. And the conditions aren't right.

You need a potent strategy to help you handle the relentless pressure of change. Something unique. Powerful. Hard-hitting enough to mobilize your group into a high performance unit. *Rapidly*.

Team ReConstruction is the high-velocity approach with the most promise. Follow these no-nonsense guidelines to shorten the high-risk transition period, protect productivity and profits, and restore the spirit of your organization.

This methodology will empower you . . . multiply your effectiveness . . . make your job easier. *Team ReConstruction* enables you to build a high performance work group even during difficult times.

PRITCHETT

Table of Contents

Face Reality.

*For now,
priority #1
is team
recon-
struction.

Why?
Because
you can't
succeed
as a
one-person
show.*

Managing a work group through major change is like running the rapids. Fighting white water.

You confront a completely new set of problems. People act differently. The world around you speeds up. There's less margin for error, but more likelihood of mistakes and a bigger price to pay if you do foul up. Many techniques that worked while you paddled along on a peaceful river no longer apply.

In the same way, shooting the rapids of organizational change means your job changes. It gets bigger. Harder. And you need to start doing different things.

The duties you prefer, or that you perform out of habit, may not matter much during transition and change. Even things you're really good at—the best skills in your managerial repertoire—may not contribute enough in times like this. Your preferred management style might be right for routine conditions, but all wrong for now.

Look at it this way. When the situation changes, so should the focus of your efforts. New problems usually call for new responses. If you fail to shift with the shifting conditions, you'll be off the mark. Even good intentions and a great effort won't get you very far if you're doing the wrong things right or the right things wrong.

This book gives you guidelines for achieving quality performance when you're working in the white water of change. These guidelines may not be consistent with your usual management style, but reality says they're right.

Another reality—for now, priority #1 is team reconstruction.

Why? Because you can't succeed as a one-person show. Top management has it right: You have to do more, with less, and do it better than before. You simply can't pull that off by yourself. You need help from the people around you. You must orchestrate a carefully coordinated group effort, achieve high quality results, and do this under very difficult conditions. Plus, you don't have time to fool around.

Don't think of team reconstruction as a distraction, or as a nuisance task over and above what you're paid to do for a living. Consider it the heart of your job. If you're too busy to carry out the tasks of team reconstruction, you're busy being wrong.

Work groups rocked by change require special attention. You must take direct aim at the destabilization. Move immediately to mobilize your team against the threats to high performance. Concentrate on engineering the individual efforts of your people into a unified, coherent, collective effort.

Reality also says you'll hit resistance. When you push to implement changes, the organization starts pushing back. Don't expect the existing culture to be on your side. More often than not, the established culture actually gets in the way during organization transitions from the old to the new. Just remember that you can't keep every employee happy, and don't get distracted trying to protect a culture that may not even be viable for the future.

Finally, the reality is that your reputation is at stake. The best way to protect that reputation is to get *results*. And that's what team reconstruction is all about.

Face reality. Do what works.

Top management has it right: You have to do more, with less, and do it better than before. You simply can't pull that off by yourself.

Empower Yourself.

Don't waste precious time waiting for a perfect set of marching orders.

If you've been assuming that superiors won't allow you to run your own show, test that assumption.

Team reconstruction takes punch. You must move with authority, make decisions, take action—you must carry influence and wield power. You can't mobilize your work group if you're immobilized yourself.

So start here: Empower yourself.

Too often, when change hits, people do just the opposite. They forfeit. Nobody strips them of their power; they give it up voluntarily simply by not exercising it. Victims of uncertainty and ambiguity, they lose their nerve, assume a "play it safe" stance, and basically disempower themselves. Higher management usually gets the blame, but these are self-inflicted wounds.

Instead of acting powerless and waiting for permission to manage, proceed as if you have all the authority you need. After all, you are the team leader.

Don't waste precious time waiting for a perfect set of marching orders. Go ahead and do what needs to be done. If you've been assuming that superiors won't allow you to run your own show, test that assumption. Rather than waiting for ideal circumstances, find out just how free you are to shape the situation the way you want it.

Frankly, top management doesn't have the time, or the inclination, to go around and re-anoint every manager and supervisor with power. Likewise, the organization can't afford the paralysis of inertia and inaction. You simply *must* empower yourself—not so you can prevail in all the power struggles, jockeying for position, or turf battles that go on, but just so you can be successful at team reconstruction.

What we're dealing with here is a mind game. This move that makes all the difference is psychological, the mental side of management. Reach deep within, for there lies the strength you need to meet the challenge of change. Empowerment, at its best, is always an inside job.

Self-empowerment may strike you as unrealistic, but it produces the most authentic power you will ever possess. Self-empowerment may seem presumptuous or risky, but it's far less threatening to your career than looking like a weakling.

Think about it. You really can't do much without power. And if you can't do much, you have no business being in charge. The team leader who looks and acts helpless won't be a leader for long. People simply won't follow a boss they don't believe in, and they won't believe in you unless you believe in yourself.

This is the time for managerial courage. A strong heart. You're going to need nerve to pull off this job of team reconstruction. Unless you have enough guts to proceed authoritatively, you weaken everyone and your work group will wallow.

Empower yourself. Only then are you in a position to empower your people.

Empowerment, at its best, is always an inside job.

Take Charge.

*You're
asking for
trouble
if you're
tentative
during
times
like these.*

Weak leadership won't work with groups that are splintered, floundering, confused, scared, angry, or dispirited. Team reconstruction calls for a management stance that inspires confidence. Change creates turmoil, and turmoil cries out for someone to take charge. Just as soldiers more readily close ranks behind a strong commander during combat, teams in transition need a leader who stands tough and has the courage of his or her convictions.

You're asking for trouble if you're tentative during times like these. If you must err, do so in the autocratic direction. Let there be no question regarding who's running the show. Leave no doubt about who's in control. Team reconstruction proceeds most successfully when it's driven hard, when the person in charge *takes charge* and makes things happen that need to happen.

Your effectiveness depends heavily on your credibility among the employees, and you undermine that credibility when you wallow, waffle, or wimp out. People won't rally behind a manager they can't respect. But don't confuse respect with popularity. Everyone in your group doesn't have to like you. Forget about being popular for now, and focus on getting results. Do what needs to be done.

Better for you to be accused of bossiness than to leave a leadership vacuum. But team reconstruction efforts are crippled if you're mean-spirited, arrogant, demeaning, or unfair in the way you deal with others. "Taking charge" doesn't justify cockiness or cruelty in the way you handle employees.

You can be authoritative without being overbearing. You can remain in control without over-controlling. You can do the hard thing without being hard-boiled. Through it all you can show care, concern, and respect for others.

Taking charge doesn't mean you have all the answers, either,

5

so be a good listener. Solicit other people's perspectives and opinions. That positions you to wield authority in an informed manner.

Your people need to have a voice, but you need to call the shots. Otherwise, you can expect anarchy. Management by committee won't work in groups that have been destabilized and reconfigured. For one thing, it's too slow a process, and you don't have any time to spare. Also, consensus management depends heavily on group agreement—something you'll find difficult to achieve, simply because people are protecting conflicting interests. There's no way you can keep everybody happy because what pleases one person disappoints the next. Each individual has a personal agenda. You'll find it impossible to reconcile them all or blend them smoothly. They're incompatible. Set your hopes on achieving consensus in a setting like this? Only a dreamer would try.

There is, of course, an important difference between effectively taking charge and being a bully. Humility has a place here. And it helps if you'll *sell* whenever you *tell*. Persuasiveness can only add to your effectiveness. Also, when you make mistakes (and you will), be quick to admit it. That's a sign of strength. It builds your credibility when you candidly acknowledge errors and press on.

Take charge. And stay in charge. Team reconstruction bogs down when people stop believing in the boss.

Your effectiveness depends heavily on your credibility among the employees, and you undermine that credibility when you wallow, waffle, or wimp out.

Set a Clear Agenda.

It stands to reason that your work group can't be effective without a clear sense of direction.

You need to step forth and set the agenda. Quickly.

Clear priorities are one of the first casualties of change. New problems compete for attention and people pursue conflicting agendas. Some previously hot projects die a sudden death, and other high priorities get put on hold. Common agreement on what most needs to be done gets lost in all the commotion and confusion.

Because of the blur, employees head in different directions, their efforts too random to produce much good. Some people simply disengage and drift, waiting for definite marching orders rather than running the risk of doing something wrong. Others may work hard individually but accomplish little collectively, proving that good intentions can result in wasted motion unless they're tightly coordinated.

It stands to reason that your work group can't be effective without a clear sense of direction. Team reconstruction stalls out when the team members spend too much time trying to figure out how to spend their time. Or when their efforts are fragmented.

You need to step forth and set the agenda. *Quickly.* Don't kill time trying to get it perfect—that could be the biggest mistake of all. As General Patton said, a good battle plan that you act on today can be better than a perfect one tomorrow.

Your plan of action should outline crystal clear tactical objectives, giving the group laser-like focus. Alignment of effort depends heavily on your ability to orient the group and orchestrate a coordinated approach.

Map out the new priorities. Keep them pure and simple. Tie them to a specific timetable. Set short-term goals that your people can achieve quickly.

You defuse a lot of potential resistance when your instructions are unequivocal, easily understood, and drilled into everybody. Even the people who don't like your plan are inclined to follow it when you make it simple, make sure every employee knows about it, and make your commitment clear.

Key subordinates often can play a meaningful role in designing the group's priorities and objectives. Consider their input. The more they get to help shape the agenda, the more buy-in and commitment they'll show. Plus, their ideas might dramatically improve your sense of priorities. In the final analysis, though, *you* remain accountable as the chief architect. Chances are the appropriate agenda can't be determined by popular vote. An overly democratic process usually inhibits team reconstruction.

No doubt you'll make adjustments in your agenda as you go along. That's just the nature of organizational change. Sooner or later you get hit with something new, or circumstances keep you from executing some of your best laid plans. That's okay. Just be sure to tell your people at the outset they can expect some mid-course corrections. Advise them to be light on their feet, because change always breeds further change.

Adapt your agenda as the situation demands it. But *always* keep it clear, and communicate it constantly. Otherwise, your team will wallow and lose precious months trying to find itself.

As General Patton said, a good battle plan that you act on today can be better than a perfect one tomorrow.

Focus on Hard Results Rather Than Intangibles.

Let's accept the fact that change affects employee attitudes. You just can't get around it. The bigger the change, the more likely you'll see it damage the way people feel toward the organization. During major upheavals the trust level drops dramatically. Morale gets mushy. Loyalty, the tie that binds, comes unravelled. Job stress hits new highs. The overall effect can be punishing, like a hard fist slammed into the stomach of the organization. And it can knock the wind out of your work group.

As the person in charge, you'd better take these emotional matters seriously. Strong feelings strongly influence people's behavior. What all this means is that your job gets a heck of a lot harder. It does *not* mean that you should make attitudinal issues such as morale, trust, and employee loyalty your top priorities. You shouldn't.

For now you should focus on problems, not symptoms. Tangibles rather than intangibles. Hard results instead of soft issues. You could waste a lot of precious time and energy chasing the wrong rainbows.

These matters of morale, trust, loyalty, and such are best thought of as *by-products*. They come about, indirectly, as a natural consequence of good management and good results. You can pursue them all you want, but you're basically just spinning your wheels unless you're managing the place right and pulling off some victories.

So don't make these intangibles the focal point of your efforts. It's not enlightened management—it's a big mistake.

What's your best bet for building trust? Simply be trustworthy in the way you have your group pursue productivity and profits. Want to help your people handle job stress? Getting rid of stressors through effective team reconstruction helps far more than concentrating on "stress training." Worried about morale and loyalty and job commitment? Watch these matters take care of themselves when the team really starts cranking. Success is the magic solution that cures so many of the "soft" organizational ailments brought on by change.

The idea here is not to diminish the importance of these intangible factors. They are vital to the long-term success of your organization. The point is simply that they should not be the "stuff" of your short-term objectives. For now your focus must be on tangible targets . . . hard results.

Shoot for the *operational* improvements that are most urgently needed. Sales gains, quicker delivery, better yields, shorter product development cycles, higher customer satisfaction, more inventory turns, fewer quality defects. Focus on stuff that heads straight to the bottom line, or that contributes directly to competitive position.

Stake out specific targets. Aim for a very few—but ambitious—goals. Go for gains you can actually measure.

Team reconstruction is a results-oriented strategy, and indirectly, it does the most to improve employee attitudes. Do a good job of team reconstruction, and you greatly improve the odds of winning. Winning, in turn, provides the most positive influence on the dispirited and disaffected.

Morale, trust, loyalty and commitment, work stress—these are very important attitudinal components. They all count. If any one of them is out of whack, the organization suffers. Collectively, they carry enough punch to make or break your work group. But you need to see them as symptoms—like fever, a headache, or nausea. And instead of popping pills or slapping on Band-Aids, you should focus on fighting the causes of those organizational aches and pains. Get rid of the root problems, and see how the unpleasant symptoms disappear. That's good medicine . . . and good management.

Shoot for the operational improvements that are most urgently needed.

Analyze Your People Assets.

Organizational change resembles a card game: shuffle, cut, and re-deal. The changes leave you with fewer people, new people, or the same people facing different challenges. For one reason or another, you need to rethink what you have to work with in terms of talent.

The casting of people—determining who goes, who stays, and who goes where—carries a lot of weight in the team reconstruction process. Put people in the right places to begin with, and you won't be forced to make shifts later on because people don't pan out. Too often reorganizations spawn further reorganizations because teams were thrown together in a haphazard manner.

Change rewrites job descriptions. So start from scratch in analyzing your available people assets. Approach the exercise as if all employees were "new hires." Even the incumbents will face new demands, and you need to evaluate their adaptability. Ask yourself if some of them should be repositioned or even eliminated. Do you have good people who are poorly suited for their positions? Should you seize this window of opportunity to eliminate lightweights or leftovers? If you can't get rid of the weaker players, at least position them where they'll hurt the team the least. Since the situation is already destabilized, the timing is right to make needed personnel moves.

Size up your crew with a dispassionate, discerning eye. You need good data, and you need to gather it in a hurry. You can't afford to sit back and figure out your people as the months go by. Eventually, of course, time would tell you who is bringing what gifts to the party, but that's a slow and expensive proposition. You need to make informed judgments *now*. If you don't trust your skills at this, or if you feel you just can't take the time, get help.

Look for strengths. Weaker points. Aspirations and work preferences. Experience and areas of expertise. Concerns and points of resistance. Be wary of the adage, "The best predictor of future behavior is past behavior." That can be a misleading notion during team reconstruction. Change has a way of bringing out the best in some people and the worst in others. Also, change has a nasty habit of causing some employees' strengths to become weaknesses, at least temporarily.

The sharper your insights into each individual, the better the odds that you'll manage him or her effectively. The more you're going on guesswork, fumbling along in the dark, the more likely you are to slot people wrong. So find the soft spots. Identify the people you'll have to shore up or work around. Recast employees whose liabilities in one position could be assets in another. Figure out who the heavy hitters are so you can play to their strengths.

You make team reconstruction harder than it has to be if you proceed with only a superficial grasp of your people assets. You also might program people for failure . . . including yourself.

Change rewrites job descriptions. So start from scratch in analyzing your available people assets.

Re-Recruit Your Keepers.

Your best promise for putting together a high-powered team comes from hanging on to your good people. When change hits, though, talent typically leaves first. Often a manager lets the most capable people get away, a setback which further complicates the task of team reconstruction.

Organizational shakeups cause most people to stop and think. Employees reassess their career progress, wonder about job security, and speculate about what the organization has to offer in the years to come. When change hits hard enough to shake their faith in the future of the organization, and in the part they'll get to play, they quickly start to consider their options.

Naturally, the best people have the most alternatives. High-talent personnel are the most likely to be recruited away and the best equipped to leave on their own initiative.

Don't assume that people are planning to stay merely because they haven't told you of any plans to leave. In fact, you should expect your best "movers and shakers" to check out other job possibilities even if you don't hear them voicing dissatisfaction with the changes. The smart money will bet on your all-stars keeping their mouths shut until they've got another job offer in their pocket.

If you wait until employees go public with their plans to leave before you re-recruit them, you've probably waited too long. When it comes to changing jobs, the heart leaves before the body. When you first hear that one of your most talented employees is thinking about leaving, there's a good chance that person already has psychologically left for a new opportunity.

Your key people can be the cornerstones of your team reconstruction effort, so don't take these people for granted. Re-recruit them. Make them feel important. Invest the same time and effort you would invest in recruiting a new employee. Sell them on the changes, on the organization, and on their roles and responsibilities in the new scheme of things.

Re-recruitment is an ongoing job for now . . . not a one-shot conversation. Give it daily attention. Just as conditions are subject to change every day, so are people's minds regarding their future.

Re-recruitment means you don't settle for merely keeping people on the payroll. You want to capture their spirit . . . put some fire into their feelings about the job . . . ensure that they're on board *emotionally* and not just showing up for work.

Success at team reconstruction depends heavily on your ability to stabilize the group. Try to keep it intact. Every time you lose a key player, you lose something else. Consider the loss of momentum, the slippage in the team reconstruction effort, if your most capable employees leave during the transition period. Think of the impact on other employees' attitudes and their confidence in the organization when your best people bail out.

You need to remember that people look at things differently during times of change. Self-preservation instincts are powerful now, and even yesterday's loyalists could be looking for greener (or safer) pastures. Start re-recruiting, so you can build from a foundation of strength in your efforts toward team reconstruction.

Often a manager lets the most capable people get away, a setback which further complicates the task of team reconstruction.

Carve Out Roles and Responsibilities.

*Let there be
no question
regarding
where one job
stops and the
next one
starts. Leave
no blur
regarding
the responsi-
bilities each
person is
supposed to
shoulder.*

Employees can't perform effectively individually, or as a team, unless they know what's expected of them. Don't leave people to figure out things on their own. Get rid of role ambiguity. Nail down every person's responsibilities with clarity, precision, and attention to detail.

Let there be no question regarding where one job stops and the next one starts. Leave no blur regarding the responsibilities each person is supposed to shoulder. Figure out precisely what needs to be done, and who's going to do which part of it, and communicate your plan.

Sounds easy, but it's not. Sounds obvious, but many managers do a half-baked job of it. As a result, they complicate life for everybody, and team reconstruction drags.

You'll feel like you're operating in an information vacuum, like your supervisors haven't given *you* the answers you need to carve out roles and responsibilities properly. Proceed anyway. Give every employee a terse but definitive job description. State your expectations regarding standards of performance. Describe the chain of command in your group. Outline each person's spending limits, decision-making authority, and reporting requirements. Both you and your employees will be best served if you get this information down in writing.

Even the employees who have been on board for a long time need these details. Even if the situation is so fluid it could change tomorrow, your team needs this information to perform well today. You can at least be specific about the short run—this day, this week, this month. And you're kidding yourself if you think you can get good results during the chaos of change *without* role clarity.

So spell it out, every bit of it. Check to make sure each person understands—not just his or her role and responsibilities, but the team's whole setup. Keep going over it until you're dead sure everyone gets the picture. See that all parties in the work group fully understand whom you've assigned to do what, and how the group fits together.

Be careful to avoid job overlap, since that feeds power struggles, wastes people resources, and frustrates the people involved. Likewise, guard against "underlap," gaps in assignments that let things slip through the cracks because no one is directly accountable.

When telling people what to do, also specify what they should *quit* doing. Some duties need to go. Differentiate between crucial tasks and peripheral, low-priority activities. Spell out what most needs to be accomplished in each position and for what the person will be held most accountable.

If you don't sharply and firmly delineate who's to do what, you have no right to complain when the situation turns into a free-for-all, or when work grinds to a halt because nobody's doing much of anything. Now is the time to take a directive stance and offer generous job structure. Work groups that are being reconfigured need a boss who will address the issues of territoriality, power and authority, and accountability. Without this kind of guidance, employees end up carrying out a random set of duties by default, and "organizational drift" sets in as the pathology of change.

Even after you carve out roles and responsibilities, pay attention to what people are doing. Keep everyone on track. You'll see some folks start trying to do somebody else's job. Not carrying their own weight. Delegating upward. Drifting back into old familiar work routines that foul up team effectiveness. When you see this, fix it. Immediately. You can't have a winning team if your people aren't playing their positions.

You're kidding yourself if you think you can get good results during the chaos of change without role clarity.

Show a Sense of Urgency.

*Some
employees
throw up
their hands
in frustration
and psycho-
logically
quit—their
bodies show
up for work
each day
but their
hearts won't
go near
the building.*

Major change breaks the rhythm of a work group. Sometimes it breaks the spirit. Productivity drags because people are confused, demoralized, angry, aimless, and worried. Some employees throw up their hands in frustration and psychologically quit—their bodies show up for work each day but their hearts won't go near the building. Other people lose their nerve, and a wary, wait-and-see attitude sets in.

This apathy and uncertainty causes people to gear down during the transition period, like a car winding its way through a construction zone. Your challenge is to rev up the group, mobilize it, and keep change from choking off its energy. Otherwise, your organization can sputter along indefinitely in the zone of team reconstruction.

You need to show some fire, a strong sense of urgency, because the employees warm by the heat of your flame. Seriously consider what your work habits say to others. Are you putting in extra hours? What about your personal productivity? Does your behavior show a burning job commitment? Without a sense of urgency, you can't function as the centering influence around which others coalesce into a team. Be a sparkplug for the group, so you don't end up in the same position as the comic strip character Pogo, who said, "I must hurry. They have gone, and I am their leader."

The best fuel for team reconstruction is the passion of the leader. Your intensity and energy. Your drive.

Take note of the cadence you personally set for your unit. As the person in charge, you have the most influence over time frames and the overall tempo of the group. People watch you intently. Like it or not, you're the role model, and employees take their cues from you.

Keep the pressure on for productivity. Set tight deadlines. Push for quicker decisions. Expedite. Operate with a bias for action.

Remember the old saying: "The pace of the leader will be the pace of the organization."

Let everybody know that you will be tolerant of honest mistakes, but intolerant of inaction and inertia. Praise the people who hustle. Nip at the heels of those who drag their feet. Get rid of the person who won't get going.

Instead of patiently planning, studying the situation, getting ready or gearing up, just get going. Move immediately to make measurable progress in a matter of months, weeks, or—preferably—even a few days. Sure, real-world limitations get in the way: attitude problems, unstable conditions, budget cuts, personnel changes . . . you name it. But you must mobilize your crew in spite of complicated circumstances.

Start with the resources at hand. Employ a fast-break offense, score quickly, and start building momentum. Inertia is your big enemy right now.

A strong sense of urgency will command the attention of others and fight their inclination to slip into a lower beat. If you allow the group to idle along, resistance to change has more time to launch a counterattack. Bureaucracy gets a better chance to bog you down. And a go-slow approach almost guarantees that your group will get hit with still more change before you finish the job of team reconstruction. That causes chronic destabilization *unnecessarily*.

The simple fact is that you don't have time to take your time. Show a sense of urgency. Team reconstruction feeds on speed.

You need to show some fire, a strong sense of urgency, because the employees warm by the heat of your flame.

Tighten Discipline.

Higher performance teams are disciplined. The team members are strict with themselves, and they execute with precision. People play for the team—not just for themselves—and are intolerant of half-hearted effort. These groups are self-policing. They deal swiftly with members who disregard the team's rule system, whether those rules are written down or just implicitly agreed on by all.

Such discipline begins to break down, though, when work groups are reconfigured and destabilized by change. For example, employees invest more energy in self-protective behavior and less in team play. The group loses its edge in coordination because people are adjusting to new roles and responsibilities. Deadlines slip as employees get distracted or have difficulty reaching decisions. "Power shifts" fuel turf battles and infighting.

Change garbles the instructions coming from the corporate culture regarding shared beliefs, rules, values, and norms. Without that tacit agreement on "how we're supposed to work together," people are inclined to follow their individual preferences in the way they go about their jobs. The group loses its ability to discipline itself, and thus becomes more "leader dependent."

For these reasons you must now function as the main disciplinary agent for your group. Until team reconstruction has been completed, until your work unit can and will police itself, the organization depends on you to bring discipline.

Start by setting high standards. Then defend them valiantly. Aim for excellence in order to build pride, esprit de corps, and cohesiveness . . . also because quality, customer service, and overall performance typically deteriorate during transitions.

Keep things tightly organized. Don't allow people to drift back into their old roles and routines. Hold employees accountable for all their assigned tasks. Keep their feet to the fire on timetables and deadlines.

Don't be vague and fuzzy in laying down the rules . . . or wishy-washy in telling people what you want . . . or inconsistent in enforcing orders. If you make as many exceptions as you do rules, you have no rules. During team reconstruction employees need consistency. Clarity. Definite limits.

Be explicit in telling employees how you will keep score. Let them know they must individually earn their keep, or they're history. Make it clear that the organization cannot tolerate resistance to change.

Be prepared to back up your words with action. People will listen to what you have to say, but their behavior will be shaped by what you *do*. If someone "breaks training"—i.e., flouts your authority, ignores the rules, or refuses to get on board—you may need to make an example out of him or her. Tough times require tough decisions. Fire one non-performer, and you'll probably *fire up* a bunch of others who suddenly begin to take you seriously.

Sound too hard-nosed to suit you? Nobody said that managing transition and change was a cakewalk. How nice it would be if things rocked along real sweetly and you never had to take heavy-duty action. But don't be surprised if some people put you in a position where *something* must be sacrificed. What are you willing to give up—an offending employee, or your credibility and authority along with the success of your team reconstruction efforts?

The bottom line is the rules must have teeth. They shouldn't be arbitrary or unfair, but during team reconstruction they should be demanding and strictly enforced.

The payoff for your efforts makes the struggle worthwhile: You'll control renegade elements, maintain respectable standards, protect productivity, and actually put your people under less stress. Above all, you greatly accelerate the process of team reconstruction.

People will listen to what you have to say, but their behavior will be shaped by what you do.

Spend Freely with "Soft Currency."

The odds are that your group members find themselves working longer and harder while having less fun. Often for the same money as before. The big question in everybody's mind is, "What's in it for me?"

Organizational change creates a climate of heightened concern. Even employees who personally benefit from the changes may be shaken by what they see happen to their comrades. Usually a pervasive sense of loss clouds the work environment. People feel more vulnerable. Even those who are initially unscathed remain uneasy about the eventual ramifications, and wait for the next shoe to fall.

You can safely assume that employees feel threatened . . . at risk . . . disempowered. These feelings demotivate your crew and interfere with team reconstruction. You need to rebuild people's confidence, restore their faith in themselves and the future. You also need to "give them something for the trouble" they're going through.

The odds are that your group members find themselves working longer and harder while having less fun. Often for the same money as before. The big question in everybody's mind is, "What's in it for me?" They feel like they're putting more into their jobs and that the rewards aren't on par with their efforts. Meanwhile, you're boxed in by the fact that you have only so much money to spend.

If you can't compensate with more cash, how will you reward good performance?

Psychological paychecks.

The intangible rewards you have to offer are limitless. Words of encouragement, compliments, empathy and understanding, a note of appreciation. Stopping to share a cup of coffee, or taking the employee to lunch. Bigger titles or special assignments. More decision-making authority. A sincere thank you. Asking about the family, celebrating small victories, soliciting opinions and suggestions. Listening . . . really listening. A mere smile, or calling the person by name. A warm handshake or pat on the back. Taking the person into your confidence. Even asking the employee for help—"needing" the person—is gratifying because it validates one's worth.

Caring, of course, takes time. It also requires you to pay attention to what's going on with your people. But caring makes a remarkable contribution to team reconstruction. Psychological paychecks have an intrinsic value that hard currency can never touch.

Create a supportive work environment—nurture—and watch it bring out the best in people. Show approval, and see how it warms the group. When you affirm, you empower. People feel safer, valued, and more optimistic. The trust level notches up. Employees show more creativity and engage their talents more fully. Psychological paychecks also build loyalty and commitment, buy the support of your people, and facilitate "bonding."

Most managers don't realize the importance that their acceptance and approval carry with subordinates. As a result, they waste this most precious resource through sheer neglect—like a bank account they never touch, money they never spend, that could be freely used to motivate and improve employees' quality of work life.

When it comes to handing out psychological paychecks, you should spend extravagantly. Your generosity will be richly rewarded. Make every team member feel special, and you'll end up with a very special team.

Psychological paychecks have an intrinsic value that hard currency can never touch.

Lay New Communication Pipelines.

Team reconstruction efforts can starve for lack of good information during transition and change. Gossip jams the circuits. The grapevine leads to information warp. Somebody drops the ball and fails to pass along data. Bosses often hole up in the office because they're so busy, or "stonewall it" because they don't have all the answers. Here and there people hoard information or deliberately twist the truth. Just when your group needs quick and accurate communication the most, good information seems hardest to get.

No doubt the communication problem extends well beyond the boundaries of your work group and pervades the entire organization. Chances are you complain about it just like your subordinates do. You'll be tempted to blame higher management, which may be justified, but that doesn't get you off the hook. Instead of waiting for others to fix the situation, start working on communication improvements that are under your control.

Give your people constant updates. Even no news is news. If you don't regularly update your employees, they'll fill in the blanks by themselves, and you feed the rumor mill by default. Unless you speak for yourself, somebody or something will speak for you.

Say things more than once if you want them to stick. Employees are hungry for information, but a lot of what management says doesn't register, never makes it into employees' memory banks. So give them a second, third, or fourth time to hear it. And if you're delivering a heavy-duty message, put it in writing.

Since communication flows four times as fast from the top down as from the bottom up, you should put new pipelines in place to carry information upstream to you. If you know what the problems are, and hear about them early enough, you can usually fix them. So deputize every employee. Tell all your people to go looking for problems. Then don't shoot the messengers who deliver bad news. Instead of looking for proof that the changes are working, search for evidence that they aren't.

Bring your group together often. Talk. Air out the issues. Pick each other's brains. Pool everyone's thoughts regarding how to resolve problems. This keeps everyone "in the loop," helps people understand each other, and keeps problems from getting out of hand.

Invite argument and allow conflict. You'll end up with better solutions. That's also the best way to identify and reconcile differences that, if swept under the rug, will come back later to haunt the group. Agreements that aren't forged out of conflict are frequently superficial. Your job is to keep issues on the table until they're resolved—the hotter the issue, the greater the need to handle it. Granted, harmony is nice, but not at the expense of effectiveness. You can't have a high performance team unless you meet the tough issues head-on.

Circulate. Talk to people . . . walk the halls . . . eat in the company cafeteria. Make contact with as many of your team members as you can. If you're out and about, you'll hear the rumors and be better able to clarify or kill them. Linger with employees a little along the way. Be approachable. Allow time for them to casually bring up their questions, suggestions, or concerns. Some of the most valuable information exchange occurs informally, so make yourself accessible.

Keep a high profile, remembering that you have no more powerful way to communicate than by example. In fact, your actions say much more than your words. This puts real pressure on you to watch what you do, because your behavior serves as the strongest statement you can make. In order for your people to pick up that message, though, you must be visible. You can't lead by example if the employees can't see you.

Be open, forthright, and honest in communicating with your team members. How you share data with them heavily influences the trust level in the group. If you're too tight-lipped, hard to read, or overly cunning, forget about getting frankness from your followers. Guardedness is pretty contagious stuff. The more selfish you are with information, the less they'll share with you.

Give your people constant updates. Even no news is news. If you don't regularly update your employees, they'll fill in the blanks by themselves.

Point Your Team Toward "Magnetic North."

Point your people in the direction of magnetic north—give them a "promised land"—and you raise their sights above the grim routine of the day-to-day grind.

Teams need to know where they're going. The players perform best when they unite with a keen sense of mission, knowing they're headed somewhere special. If the aiming point is clear and the "vision" is compelling, it draws the people together and pulls them forward.

The dream serves as magnetic north, swinging the needle of the group's attention away from the demoralizing aspects of "now" to the inspiration of "what could be." For teams mired in an unpleasing present, fearing a bleak future, or clinging to the past, this mental shift is critical. Forward movement comes easiest when people are attracted to what they're moving toward.

Point your people in the direction of magnetic north—give them a "promised land"—and you raise their sights above the grim routine of the day-to-day grind. Offer something besides a salary to sustain them through the trials of change, something that touches them deep within and justifies the struggle. A shared vision can engage the heart . . . fire commitment . . . glue the group together.

In defining magnetic north for your team, concentrate on making it a *cause*. People get fired up about crusades, but not about "strategic plans." A vision is more like a *movement* than like a dry set of corporate financial objectives.

Paint your team's "promised land" in vivid color. Use bold strokes. Make it an image with enough magnetic pull to grab everyone's attention and compelling enough to overpower resistance to change. Then keep holding the picture up for your people to see. Promote the vision constantly. Keep it alive in their minds.

Your work group must have a purpose if it is to move purposefully. Without one, individuals drift, go their separate ways, lose sight of the logic behind collective effort. Without a vision of something better to shoot for, hope fades. People start thinking, "This is it . . . this is as good as it's gonna get," not realizing that they are viewing the future from a trough instead of a mountaintop.

Use your imagination. Get creative. Come up with something dramatic enough to stir the souls of your people. Even if it has to be short-range, they need a sense of mission that serves them all as a common aiming point for their efforts.

Any group or subgroup, however small, is free to draw up a vision that represents its own magnetic north. Ideally, smaller units will synchronize theirs with that of the parent organization, but they also can proceed independently if the parent has left a void in this respect. Don't put this task on the back burner even if higher management hasn't told you what to shoot for. You may never get clear signals from them.

You're trying to reconstruct a team, mobilize a coherent and dynamic group effort, and your people need a mission they can get passionate about. So take the initiative. Give them a sense of purpose that captures their imagination and encourages them to close ranks. Team reconstruction accelerates dramatically when the members buy in to the dream and move together toward magnetic north.

A shared vision can engage the heart . . . fire commitment . . . glue the group together.

Pay Attention to Process.

Think of *process* as your organization's gearbox, the internal machinery of how it goes about its business. When change hits, the gears of this machinery start grinding. The quality of teamwork suffers. This is a common problem during transition and change, and it calls for special attention.

Destabilized teams need to be self-monitoring. Self-correcting. But during times of transition, team members are notorious for sidestepping or overlooking the problems of group process. Most employees are looking out for themselves rather than for the team. People are so busy "doing" that they don't take time to appraise how they're going at it. Sometimes they lack confidence in the group's ability to handle the stress of self-analysis, so they don't force the issue.

The result? Nobody calls attention to dysfunctional process, and it slows team reconstruction.

As the person in charge, you should focus attention on process. Watch what's going on inside the group. Analyze its effectiveness. Determine what's missing, what's getting in the way, what needs to happen. You need a sharp eye plus enough guts to confront the group and make it deal with the process problems.

Stop the team in its tracks. Regularly. Call a halt long enough to let the group hold a mirror up to itself. Process analysis is as simple as saying, "Let's look at what's going on here. Now. How do you feel about that? Let's analyze how we're working together as a group."

This exercise is a lot like a half time locker room review, where the football coach and his players take a few minutes to critique how the game is going and make important adjustments. When your group gets bogged down, call timeout. Make everybody huddle and take a hard look at what's happening. Don't let people dodge the tough issues, gloss over sensitive points, or turn the conversation toward mere chitchat. Make them face the facts and come up with constructive ideas on how to handle the process problems. Keep them cornered until they identify and *deal* with the problems in how they're working together. The situation can get tense, but you're headed for bigger problems if you let them off the hook. Go ahead and put them through the drill.

Process analysis is powerful stuff. It can turn the game around when team reconstruction seems to be a losing battle. Even if things seem to be humming along just fine, stop periodically to critique how things are working. High performance teams always pay attention to process.

The results you produce on the job will be shaped as much by group process as by the raw talent on your team. Even highly competent individuals who are committed and hardworking can't succeed as a group if their efforts are unsynchronized, inefficient, or off target. Team performance depends on how well the group uses its resources, manages its time, communicates, makes decisions, solves problems, interfaces with other groups, stays focused. What goes on inside the work unit heavily influences its output.

Make it clear that every person is in charge of protecting group process. Tell everyone to throw the spotlight of attention on behavior that gets in the way.

One of the prescriptions for successful team reconstruction is constant diagnosis, relentless scrutiny of the group's internal operations.

You need a sharp eye plus enough guts to confront the group and make it deal with the process problems.

When it seems you have things under control, and you feel the task of team reconstruction is complete, take a breather. You probably deserve it.

Mainly, though, you need to catch your breath and get ready to go again.

There's more white water ahead.

Price Pritchett

Ron Pound

T R A I N I N G

TEAM RECONSTRUCTION

Program for Managers

Destabilized organizations hunger for leadership. They respond best to take-charge management, to leaders who kick into gear with the special moves it takes to mobilize people and protect productivity during change.

Team ReConstruction gives leaders a high-velocity approach to help their work groups recover from "change shock" and deliver impressive results. Participants learn how to counter the ambiguity and uncertainty, retain talent, bring order out of confusion, and inspire high performance under difficult conditions.

Agenda
Module 1: Climate for *Team ReConstruction*
Module 2: Take Charge/Focus on Tangible Results
Module 3: Analyze Your People Assets
Module 4: What Now?

Key Objectives
- Learn to mobilize teams for greater productivity during change
- Identify situations that demand "take-charge" leadership
- Focus on tangible results to boost morale and rebuild trust

Topics Addressed
- How change damages team performance
- 3 *Team ReConstruction* strategies and why they work
- Identification and analysis of different team roles, behaviors, and their importance
- Individual action plans to accomplish tangible results for the team

Primary Result
Participants learn how to meet the new leadership challenges created by change. They identify their own contribution to the team and learn to value the contribution of other team members as well. Action plans are created for building a high performance work group that will maintain productivity and ensure success.

For more information on our quick-impact training,
or to order additional handbooks
call 800-992-5922
or order online at www.pritchettnet.com

BOOKS BY PRITCHETT, LP

- *After the Merger: The Authoritative Guide for Integration Success**

- *Business As UnUsual: The Handbook for Managing and Supervising Organizational Change**

- *Carpe Mañana: 10 Critical Leadership Practices for Managing Toward the Future*

- *Culture Shift: The Employee Handbook for Changing Corporate Culture**

- *The Employee Guide to Mergers and Acquisitions**

- *The Employee Handbook for Organizational Change**

- *The Employee Handbook for Shaping Corporate Culture: The Mission Critical Approach to Culture Integration and Culture Change**

- *The Employee Handbook of New Work Habits for a Radically Changing World**

- *The Employee Handbook of New Work Habits for The Next Millennium: 10 Ground Rules for Job Success*

- *The Ethics of Excellence*

- *Fast Growth: A Career Acceleration Strategy*

- *Firing Up Commitment During Organizational Change**

- *Hard Optimism: Developing Deep Strenghts for Managing Uncertainty, Opportunity, Adversity, and Change**

- *High-Velocity Culture Change: A Handbook for Managers**

- *The Leadership Engine: Building Leaders at Every Level,**
Based on Noel Tichy and Eli Cohen's best-selling hardcover from HarperBusiness, a division of HarperCollins Publishers. Introduction by Price Pritchett.

- *Making Mergers Work: A Guide to Managing Mergers and Acquisitions**

- *Managing Sideways: A Process-Driven Approach for Building the Corporate Energy Level and Becoming an "Alpha Company"**

- *The Mars Pathfinder Approach to "Faster-Better-Cheaper": Hard Proof From the NASA/JPL Pathfinder Team on How Limitations Can Guide You to Breakthroughs*

- *Mergers: Growth in the Fast Lane**

- *MindShift: The Employee Handbook for Understanding the Changing World of Work*

- *Outsourced: 12 New Rules for Running Your Career in an Interconnected World*

- *The Quantum Leap Strategy*

- *Resistance: Moving Beyond the Barriers to Change*

- *Service Excellence!**

- *Smart Moves: A Crash Course on Merger Integration Management**

- *A Survival Guide to the Stress of Organizational Change**

- *Team ReConstruction: Building a High Performance Work Group During Change**

- *Teamwork: The Team Member Handbook**

- *you^2: A High-Velocity Formula for Multiplying Your Personal Effectiveness in Quantum Leaps*

---

*Training program also available. Please call 800-992-5922 for more information on our training or international rights and foreign translations.

Team
ReConstruction

1-49 copies	____ copies at $6.95 each
50-99 copies	____ copies at $6.50 each
100-999 copies	____ copies at $5.95 each
1,000-4,999 copies	____ copies at $5.75 each
5,000-9,999 copies	____ copies at $5.50 each
10,000 or more copies	____ copies at $5.25 each

Please reference
special customer number 55TR
when ordering

Name _____

Job Title _____

Organization _____

Address _____

Country _____ Zip Code _____

Phone _____ Fax _____

Email _____

Purchase order number (if applicable) _____

Applicable sales tax, shipping and handling charges
will be added. Prices subject to change.
Orders less than $250 require prepayment.
*Orders of $250 or more may be invoiced.

☐ Check Enclosed   ☐ Please Invoice*

☐ VISA   ☐ MasterCard   ☐ AMERICAN EXPRESS

Name on Card _____

Card Number _____ Expiration Date _____

Signature _____ Date _____

TO ORDER
By phone: 800-992-5922
Online: www.pritchettnet.com
Call for our mailing address or fax number.

PRITCHETT
Dallas, Texas